JANUARY  WITHDRAWN

Also by Peter Sansom from Carcanet

Everything You've Heard Is True

Peter Sansom

JANUARY

CARCANET

Acknowledgements

Poems in this collection were first published in: *The Green Book*, The *Guardian*, *Lampshade* (Huddersfield Polytechnic), *Instead of a Journey* (Holmfirth Writers), *London Magazine*, *Poetry Review*, *PN Review*, *The Rialto*, *Slow Dancer*, *SW Arts Competition Anthology*, *Verse* and *The Wide Skirt*.

I am grateful for an Arts Council Writer's Bursary in 1992 and for a similar award from the Society of Authors in 1993.

First published in 1994 by
Carcanet Press Limited
Conavon Court
12-16 Blackfriars Street
Manchester M3 5BQ

A CIP catalogue record for this book
is available from the British Library.
ISBN 1 85754 086 7

The publisher acknowledges financial assistance
from the Arts Council of Great Britain

Set in 10 pt Caslon 540 by Bryan Williamson, Frome
Printed and bound in England by SRP Ltd, Exeter

Contents

I Opened the Door

I opened the door and walked through.
I opened the door and stood in the doorway.
I opened the door and hit my head on the edge.
I cut my head open opening the door.
I opened the door no problem,
I have been opening doors all my life, as long as I can remember.
I opened the door and went out,
It was raining.
I opened the door and went out,
It was sunny.
I opened the door and it wasn't raining or sunny,
It was a cupboard door.
I couldn't open the door it was locked.
I couldn't open the door it was bolted on the inside.
I couldn't open the door it was a window.

January

You stand at the door (you sometimes are
the door) and, according to tradition, look
to the past year as well as to the new;
but me, I'm all for that watch, moving on
in a room so quiet I can almost see
the second finger as it beats against each mark,
though for a while I can't place it,
there, by the blank appointments book and diary
on the uncluttered desk. Mid-morning
the beginning of 1993.
We have been to the coast, as we do.
The garlands are down, the tree undressed
and hoovered under, bin-bagged and put out.

2
According to tradition, and by name,
you look back as you look forward, while what is
is people skating on their arses down Slant Gate,
burst pipes, a broken tanker spilling oil,
or the fox's single line of prints
to scramble our ice-locked gate for scraps
we first of all put out for the birds.
Now we put out rind, bread, apples at night,
for him, always the same young fox.

3
Reading by candlelight, next door's telly
on with this year's honours, I saw you,
at that moment, or thought I did, on a long slow track
out of evergreen woods, the start
of a ridge walk between two counties
when the valley was a stopped snowstorm
and the mountain air was white in our lungs
all morning gradually higher and higher,
my friend and I, what great friends we were then.
Till, reaching a summit, we could look down
with all of nature in our English pocket
and point out scree and gullies, scattered homes,
and name the named mountains round us
before picking our way back to the pinched-grey lake,
the straggling winter village, the mini-mart and café.
I saw you all right, but your back was turned.

4

Young and old, you give voice to a bell
telling midnight across an estuary,
crossed, uncrossable, the air thick with salt;
and that voice has the gawky confidence
of sharp bright metal; but that voice too
is the round, sober parish bell, the copper tang
of licking an old penny. Its chimes roll by
to where you are; and, at the last of them,
you are here, unassuming, a fox
in that fable of the old fox in his cave,
pretending to be ill and inviting
all the animals to visit him
so he could eat them without having to go out.

By the Canal at Linthwaite

I am not a fisherman, and only lately
have the nerve – without the kids – to sit
on a drizzling towpath while the wooden sailboat
tacks out across and under the birches'
leaning darkness at the far bank. I love it.

There are mallard there, stock-still
in the shadow, the chameleon dusk. Cast bread
or so much as take out one slice
and even as you break it, still in your hands,
they come, patient, direct as if motorized.

The little boat is nothing to them, not food
nor threat; its dowelling boom swings over
at a twitch on the line that follows
it everywhere, fastened to the fore,
bringing it gamely into the breeze.

It makes good speed back through real waves
at that scale, dashed now with a simmering
downpour. And me out in that weather,
sailing a toy boat, not even thinking,
just looking at the water.

The Reader

I have come to read
he said to my opened door, my incidental form there.
His shadow fell into the hallway
as he stepped by me
holding a pass, a blue card, which he showed me
and saying *Shall I go through*
he went through.
Thorough, at speed, he read
the spines of the record collection
and the tapes, the absence of cds;
he turned to read for a moment the fire,
and the mantelpiece, its plants, framed photo,
scented candles, the wide mirror above it.
He read the kitchen shelves and the herb rack,
the fridge, the pots and pans,
he read the cat bowl and the radio dial
he read the crockery.
In the playroom he read the numbers
round the dartboard and the names
on the books in alphabetical, no other order,
fiction or philosophy, history or ancient history.
He read all the postcards.
He read the telephone and its notepad
then, loosening his tie, shrugging off his jacket,
he sat to begin the desk diary,
which took him some little time,
all the while reading with his fingers
the pittings and rings from cups and glasses,
he read a straightened paperclip.
Returning, he thumped the sofa back
and read the dust in the watery sun
in at the picture window
and the entire valley beyond it.

A Stone in a Drystone Wall

I have lived so long in this wall
I might have been born here. My family
sit round me, hold me in, hold me up,
fallen once, built back.
At night the cold and often the rain.
I can feel it, it is not pure.
Part of me is gone, worn away
for the sake of a boundary,
for the sake of keeping one man's sheep
from another man's grass: little more
than scrubland that after all
would be stronger for cropping.

It is still night. I am aware of the stars
as I am of the seasons, though only for a moment
over the line of forest from my crammed-in
angle do I ever see a star.
I cannot imagine which constellation it belongs to.
It is dimmed and flickers
but never quite disappears.
Mostly I remember a time there was daylight,
the sun coming up like a promise honoured
and being warmed by it.

Tree

I have heard tell of a dream,
and of the man who woke from it
with the stars at the window
and frost over the field
that sloped to his blue back door.

In that dream I am nameless
and without family.
I am not Oak nor Ash nor Yew
nor Holm nor Holly, though he
would have me all of these,
the parent-tree or representative
known by *the shape and profusion*
of my glossy dark-green leaves.

*

He shivered, washed, and dressed
in his best suit, charcoal,
bought for a wedding and for a funeral,
and worn at both, days apart, one winter;
and a white, ironed shirt
from his linen drawer;
black shoes; a grey tie. He looked out
for a while at the hill that was
and was not the hill in his dream.

At length he knelt
to set a match to the fire.
Everything was ready. He remembered,
and switched on at its neck
a lamp that made the window
four portions of a wall of books,

and, as the dream had showed him,
he chose a volume from the centre,
and opened it, and read my story,
as I shall now relate:

*

'My thought returns to the parish
that cut me down, without warning, without prayer,
so clumsily, it took two men
and their sharp axes an hour.
I fell by degrees, bending with each hurt
until I was torn from the roots,
and dragged across uneven pasture to a lane
that winds slowly up by a working farm.
There they paused to wipe their faces
and unpeel their sticking shirts.

They listened to the animals in their stalls,
and pointed to the first colour in the east.
Then, complaining at my stubborn weight,
they lifted me again to attack the hill.

                    *

Eventually it was morning,
and there was the committee, waiting.
The Lord Mayor and the county Sheriff,
some from the church and some local traders,
soldiers in crisp khaki, joking;
and two anxious, out-of-place chippies

who, at once, at a signal, against time,
set to work. By mid-morning, I knew
what I would be: a gibbet. By midday
I was it, to swing *the man who poached a hare,
or rode away another's chestnut mare,
and the boy who took his best friend's life
in one simple lunge of a kitchen knife.*

And there I should have stayed,
recalled as a warning
in tales round the fire on winter evenings.

                    *

When at once I was incandescent
in light unknown till then,
flame without heat, fire without burning
and across my crossbeam shone
five jewels, five little, precious stones,
ruby-droplets that glimmered and were gone.

The prisoner stepped up to me,
and turned to the assembly.

Not the noose, at this,
so skilfully looped to me

but the sergeant and his men at a command
hoisted him on to me –
a man made by that motion into a cross,
his uncomplaining arms, his open hands
while another, hooded, swiftly,
with one sharp stroke, hammered
a thin stake through his left wrist, then
unflinching through his right,
and lapped his feet together
and joined them also with a stake.

Then it was nightfall and we were alone.
The stars turned above us and I held him on my arms.

*

At dawn they came and wrenched him
from me. He bled no more, and the blood
had dried – but he was not dead,
though they shouldered his corpse,
and carried it from me, a sullen crowd round them,
down the valley to the green, out of sight
by the shining roofs of their cottages,
the first wisps of woodsmoke.

And, as it might have been Market day,
so many travelled this early
the moor from each direction,
or else as it might be the day
of a fair or the midwinter feast:
more then, steadily, and still more of them,
on horseback or leading horse and trailer,
with goods and chattels, or singly, and with music,
or on foot and driving cattle, and there
an orderly flock of sheep prodded on;
working men and women and children
in bright clothes and singing
as they strode across the rushing grasses
toward town as if to some great, happy ceremony,
as if to some great, joyous festival.'

Above 1,000ft, Anyone without an Ice Axe and Instep Crampons

is a bloody fool. Us, for instance,
with a large-scale O.S. but too idle
to get it out and trace the broken line
off one fell and up to the point
of our walking, Blea Cragg. But that isn't
the point, which is to be here, men
among mountains that might be the Andes;
taking turns to step in each other's tracks
which give up to the thigh, any moment
to dislodge shingle under your boots
or my stout but split Dr Marten shoes.
It's then you'd need the ice-axe to bring down
hard and hang on to. 'A third leg,' a climber
told us last night, 'for walking at altitude';
and you, 'Tell that to Leon Trotsky.'

The sheep are more sure-footed, frightened
down bivouac folds, across snow-fields,
towards that ridge we take to be Great Gable,
but we could be wrong. There is something heroic
about being stupid, more than likely
lost this high, no compass, no whistle
(though we know the emergency signal),
and the packed lunch and survival kit
forgotten back at the Hostel
with the Swedish or Danish girl you thought
might come across: the surprise, walking
in the showers and finding her, naked
and with enough English to say *Gentlemen*.

We speculate on what might have been, once,
and from there get round to the girls
at college we fooled with or who broke our hearts,
as we step below the snow line to what might be
Buttermere or who knows Borrowdale.
Now it is a wider path, till stopped
by a puddle: practically a pool, big enough
to hold a whole tree. And there too
under the daft bobble hats our wives chose,
superclearly among white sky
and black branches, our blank red faces.

Lake

If I didn't look up,
the lake went on forever, like one of those lakes
we heard so much of

from that teacher
from Ontario. You pulled back smartly and my book
obedient to physics

lifted, pulling me
back. The rowlocks creaked where they were splintering
and there was a

rising inch of water,
but it was safe enough and hot enough if not.
In any case, soon

behind the island,
we'd break the rule and swim from the boat.
It was something

to be held by ripples
through an afternoon whose two-hour hire had only
just begun.

The novel I read out
made room in the last century for us, though we knew
how the love-match

must end, since whatever
the obstacles or tracks of possibility those heroines
always got their man.

We took turns,
but you loved rowing, being in control; and I liked
being passenger

on that cool
upswelling water – the vivid drops from the lifting tip
of the oar, the

hollow splash
as you struck, pulling us on; until, far enough out,
and though the sun

had drifted behind cloud
I'd put the book down and the struggle from our shorts and
tee-shirts would

nearly capsize us,
until, gasping even before we slid into the water, we
abandoned ship.

At Blea Tarn

The water goes nervously off
as you paddle in the shallows.
It is mild for February but even so
and this fell two miles above Grasmere
is public. It is midmorning.
You are not drunk. We have not
just pedalled out of rime-cast bivvy-bags
and put a blue windchoked flame
under the half-pint kettle.
We have strolled up here from a youth hostel.
You are not sixteen. There are no girls to impress.
You are shivering, white, determined.
How to explain your nakedness
under this grey sky, numb up to your knees
in that clear black water?

I remember two or three summers
how we'd swim from a hired boat on Grasmere;
and at the end of a high-walled orchard
how you'd strip to sunbathe,
and once read your book like that
through a storm under the dripping trees.
But this is something else. I feel my heart
clench as you stride now splashing deeper in
until you're swimming, swimming.

Skating

There is a lake, gathering flurries
of snow; and the lake is black, frozen,
and those beautiful birds ungainly
slapstick trying to land or take to the air.
There are four or five people in bright colours,
trailing scarves, skating like the Dutch,
hands behind backs, swiftly round.

Your eyes become accustomed to the dark.
The stars are unusually bright.
There is fairground music, faintly,
and on the far shore people;
where, by the jetty, boats are locked
into their moorings, and just beyond
are the bonfires and dancing.

You have come all this way,
then trekked a mile, maybe two
through forest from the car.
So you sit on a tree stump
and do up the laces; blow into
your gloves and slip them back on.
The music and the skaters' voices

reach you more clearly. You fumble
your glasses into their case
and into a pocket, then zip
your windcheater up, and
on borrowed skates half a size too small,
and pulling your bobble hat right,
you waddle on to the ice.

Aldeburgh

We turn our backs on the sinister green light
at Sizewell and trudge along the pebble beach,
the flat water unhurried, despite a breeze
that chivvies our crunching steps. To our left
a moon comes to the full just beyond
the horizon of the sea. We are walking
from the guest-house the wrong way,
though we won't know it till later,
to a party that is part of the carnival.
'Carne Vale,' you say: 'farewell to flesh'
replacing steel drums with a danse macabre;
'for Lent,' you add, though it is November,
and I think of the rail link to Saxmundham
still running, but only for plutonium.
Nearer, we see that those mutations
are anglers behind huge umbrellas. One stands
to cast again, and we change our path; and then
another towards us, who seems to clamber
from the sea, a lost soul inside his own
travelling arctic glow, a halogen lamp,
and burdened with tackle, going home. We cross back
to the metalled road, still in no hurry.
In a meteor storm, it occurs to me to say,
you might make any number of wishes.
You stop and look up, as anyone would,
at the moon and the motionless stars.
You are my wife, but that's not why I love you.

Canal

You walk from one West Riding village
to another, and what you see there,
what you recall, is yours for an hour
and ours, if we look to it, for ever.
You walk, wearing out some shoe-leather,
by bindweed and late nettles brittle
with frost (though the afternoon feels mild).
And where the canal drags at lock gates
you see the windows of a dyeworks' warehouse
as stretched and bordered squares of darkness
sunk in water green-lighted from within
by rich, industrial effluent;
water not water but standing so thick
that anyone might almost walk on it.
You take a stone to throw at that
topsy-turvy image of glass in water,
and its ripples break out smoothly,
almost unnoticed, almost perfect.

Soon it's time to turn from this anywhere
you know and care for. The sky is clear
but darkening with colours that the sun drains
beyond a far, sprawling hill. House lights
appear on it like early stars, too remote
to name, or read anything in their pattern.
It is getting chilly. You pause to cup a flame
to a small cigar, turn up your collar and,
half-across a packhorse bridge, look down
at the stopped water. Already
you are thinking of the short walk back
along a main road to your car,
the car keys already in your hand.

My friend, you are too private a person
for me to see you further on your way:
what do I know of you, and how presume,
in something of your own manner, but without
your gift and discipline, to speak of you,
whose writings I learned most from
and value most. Beside that passionate
dispassionate exactness I measure
all too clearly my shortcomings in this

as in most other things. Nevertheless
I have made this for you, empty gesture
though it is, anonymous between a student
and his teacher; between the living and the dead;
a gesture like wiping away tears, and too modest
to call itself grief, let alone love.

Chair

All right, so let's start this one again
about the chair in the front room and the man
trapped there. At any time he might get to his feet.
The kettle clicks off. The chain stops the door.
At any time he might get up.
He is not a doll in that chair.
He is not a guy in his own cast-offs
to burn less brightly each year.
But he does not get up.
The television is everywhere and always on.
An old woman with the rough of her tongue
will dress and feed him and his son.
Sometimes the chair is on the verandah
with plastic marble tubs, hanging baskets
a washing line, the neighbourly adjacent flats.
But always in the end the chair is in the room
with rarely all of us and almost never alone.
It is 1919, the morning of his first job,
already late and a dog crashes through
the window to go with him. It is the '50s,
late again in the street with some nonsense
for the gaffer who would sack him if he could.
By the middle '60s he's laid off
early with his back. Off up the allotments
or the Labour Club or the Soldiers and Sailors
but mainly in that chair, waited on.
What can I tell you except he'll never be dead
as long as I am alive, and those last years,
when a can of stout made blood,
I understand them too as a sort of laziness,
a line from a hymn repeated and a dog bark
when he can't stop talking and he can't make sense.

Mittens

I am wearing mittens.
I've not worn mittens since Infants,
can still smell the stink of the toilets,
still feel the grey thick-painted cloakroom pegs.
I don't know if there was string to them then
but there's string to these,
a couple of metres threaded through the sleeves.
The coat is bright blue.
The mittens are red, hand-knitted.
I'd forgotten how hard it is to grip in mittens.

She tucks my scarf in and fastens
the last toggle. 'Stand up straight.
Don't pull faces, you'll stop like it.'
She brushes my hair. 'There.'
We are by the back door now. It is smaller,
almost so that I have to bend.
It still sticks. 'Wait,' she says, and
bows my face to hers, 'you can't go out like that.'
She licks her hankie, and rubs
at the stubble on my cheek I must have missed.

Settee in Autumn

The leaves change colour and fall
on the russet settee.

Sticky buds are stuck
down the back of the settee with coins and old biros.

The last, unpicked blackberries
are left to rot on the settee.

A little acorn is starting the long, almost
motionless journey to becoming a mighty settee.

The first frost has set in on the settee.

Three tins of Weightwatcher Tomato Soup are brought
to the harvest festival on the settee.

All across the country, anti-freeze is poured into settees
but still in the dark mornings many settees refuse to start.

Jump leads are attached to settees
and settees are pushed by neighbours up the street.

Dank mists; the sparkling spider's web
is filigree on the settee.

Two Die in Apple-Bobbing Drama on Settee.

There are fir-cones among the outrageous springs
and horsehair in the settee.

There is a pumpkin head on the settee.
There is Guy Fawkes on the settee.

There are settees on settees
on the blazing bonfire of the settees.

A Wood

A wood, traditional.
It is a part
of my waking life, too.
If it has colour,
I am colour blind.
There is no warden,
there is a gardener.
Among the close trees,
the needles are cleared
regularly, swept into bags
by children in the holidays.
Frail plants flourish
despite the darkness.
The topmost branches
break on each other
in the north-easterly,
though where we stand
it is silent, like a room
left to its own devices,
cleared till the contracts
are sealed and delivered
and the new couple move in
with their different taste

unmuffling the floorboards
wall to wall to sand them.
They sit long nights and talk
to each other, not conversation
but speeches, word-perfect.

We listen to them now.

On Not Being Mr Dugan

He was not an ordinary ghost
or I will have to revise my ideas
about ghosts. Broad day; I banked the fire
against the warmest January in years,
for the look of it. The flame burnt blue.
I went for no reason and looked out
in time to see him walk from the sea,
the sun too weak to cast a shadow
as he climbed the steps under my window;
and when I opened to his knock
his clothes were clean dry linen,
and his sandy hair, his beard were dry.
Will you ask me in of your own free will?
The most natural thing in the world.

I thank you, he said, and sat by the fire
took the glass and drank it off.
Cold, he said, as I poured him another.
You will be young Mr Dugan, at last,
and I nodded. You have come back, I ventured,
and that was a damn fool question.
My next, for his name and his story, the same.
He was silent then, a quarter of an hour,
watching the fire, or asleep I thought.
You are not Mr Dugan, he concluded.

He had a mind to eat. Surprised, I said of course,
going through, and asked (he stank like a barn)
would he like a bath, but ghosts abhor water,
except a little in a lot of whisky.
I've had water enough, he said.
Later, What can you show me, he said
so I switched on the lamp, dull in the sun,
and turned on the telly and the video.
But he had seen these things and they were nothing,
A very bourgeois achievement, he said.
I wondered where he'd learned that word bourgeois.
It seemed he had done a deal of walking,
aimless walking such as his people recommend,
and he poured the last of the whisky, and sat back.

I made coffee, and asked again for his story.
He put his feet up on the nest of tables
and began as you'd expect with the murder:
pitched in the sea by the second mate,
from a boat in sight of the whale, and only
six to the boat against that animal.
He was murdered for a female he waylaid
last time in port. Pitched overboard
and not drowned, but died at once of the cold.
'Was this Dugan your murderer then?' He sat up.
It was not, Sir, Mr Dugan, the kindest man
to walk God's earth. You'd not catch him
killing a man while his back was turned.
He'd do it to your face and with a knife
or his bare hands. And he would too. He'd seen it.
'And the second mate, the murderer?'
He didn't remember, it didn't matter:
he'd had the wench, still in her petticoat
from the second mate's visit
and his picture portrait looking on.

He talked some more about the woman
and about his wife and a girl called May.
I asked, Who is this Mr Dugan?
He shook his head. Look now at the harbour.
There was a dog, a black labrador
rocking into the water. 'Surely not.'
And it certainly is *not*, he said;
but he'd take his leave for all of that:
the tide was turning. 'Will you come back?'
For sure, he said, but not to you.
'Before you go,' I said, 'won't you tell me
something about the other world?'

'Well mine,' he said, 'is damned wet
and damned cold.' And pitch black too, I expect,
I said, to detain him. 'No, no,' he said, turning
at the door. 'It is a very pleasing colour,
and I'll tell you another thing: one morning
you will wake there, and fluent as a native.
Me,' he said, 'it is still a foreigner to.
What is your name, Sir?' When I told him,
he asked was I sure, and shook his head again.
And your name? I said, but already

he was struggling back down the steps
and already was there on the steep path
to the private beach, across the sand
without a backward look. I watched him
as without pausing he walked into the sea
and went on walking, with one of the pier lights
calm on the dark surface through
his lumbering shape, until he was gone.

At the Market

At the market they are selling
All the goods you ever wanted
And all the girls are willing
For the money in your purse.

If you've the wherewithal to buy it
You can get yourself a soapbox
To spout from down the market
Though your stammer's getting worse.

You've not seen that market movie
Because of course you're *in* it –
You're on the cover and the telly
And make a million from your verse.

At the market though their potions
And strategic lifts and implants
Can't stop the ageing process,
They can put it in reverse.

But beware: talent is no asset
At the market; if you make it
You'll have to stuff your ears with money
When the jealous buggers curse.

Yet when you croak it on the market
And you're finally laid to rest
It is on the gorgeous breast
Of a really private nurse

And the whole nation in mourning
Comes trailing round the market
With love and praise for the bunting
And history for your hearse.

Fame

How could anyone sleep with all that
happening in their head, not to mention the fleas,
and outside so much trees, wind and rain
as the beginning of the flood again.

I pad in just a shirt down the loud stairs
and squint at the clock by blue gas:
four-thirty at the setting to boil
of a shallow kettle in December.

Yesterday somebody rang the office
to see if I'd killed myself. He was surprised
at my voice, yes, but I only imagined
the disappointment. And really it was

an easy mistake, and anyone could have made it,
reading the obituary of a man who worked
where I once worked, a writer hardly anyone
had read, and who was hurt by that,

or so the paper said. He congratulated me,
that acquaintance, on my continuing existence,
and we thought, briefly, of the other man,
my age, my height, same colour eyes.

No Plot

Things just as they happened.
The sergeant major, the joker, the mate
who would lay down his life –
each in turn is abandoned
or killed off.

It starts with the narrator
lying about his age
and ends four years later
with him stretchered back
three weeks before VE Day.

He'll be seventy-three or four
next month – he loses track.
Already the son-in-law
is talking about a home.
They think he is losing his grip.

His great ambition, this
crisply-written, intelligent book.
A dozen publishers have seen it,
half a dozen agents.
There is no market.

He wants to know, so I talk
about developing character
and using the setting;
about showing, not telling;
how in fiction

everything has meaning.
I am the professional.
He weighs me up, carefully,
and sits back down:
he will give me

a free hand
and a share of the royalties
if I can make it right.

Translating Hans Carossa

I put a new plant in the window like a lamp,
the last light of spring in winter,
and look out at the garden full of rain
which by morning will be settled snow;
turn to your book and the dictionary
and imagine what others made of you.

By midnight I wonder where the evening went,
and what it was I *did* at school.
For the last hour, the radio still
on with Baghdad, I sit with coffee and brandy
over *An Atlas of the Heavens*,
learning the constellations, clusters
of individual names. Only on cloudless nights
do I ask myself what use it is.

You saw too much destruction,
And if the cathedral in your town
Was left standing, that was no Act of God;
And though the steeples survived
Close to the wind-blown cloud,
Already something was flying to them
To lift them from their equilibrium:
The bells called out one last time as

The whole shooting match bit by bit collapsed:
A Weltanschauung *one day to be replaced*
By a stronger argument, clearer,
And more persuasive, as most wrong theories are.

Altar and nave became sepulchre and tomb.
The graves themselves were blown to kingdom come.

The Old Fountain

after Hans Carossa

Put your book down, put the light out
and go to sleep. That noise is only
the fountain in the courtyard. You'll get used to it,
everybody does. Until, in the middle
of a dream about your journey here –
the pine-forest, the lake, the hissing roads –,

a restlessness will run through the house;
and you'll wake to silence and the ghost
of footsteps up the gravel drive. Don't worry.
It's only somebody with a long way to go
cupping his hands, getting a drink.

Soon the water will be running again as if
he'd never been here. Look at it this way:
it proves you're not alone. Look at it
this way: a lot of people have drunk
at that fountain over the years.
And don't think there won't be others.

Poem

The small car made the bend ok, the bridge,
but came to rest nearly vertical
at a lamp-post whose timer and lamp
were out, the radiator crumpled but the
chassis intact, for all the world a car
that had decided for its own amusement
and ours to climb a post and get the right
angle to turn its clear-eyed headlights
into searchlights picking out
snowflakes as they swirled in their fall.

A Dream Mistaking a Person for
What He Has Come to Represent

When Ted Hughes stayed at our house
he fried himself a full English breakfast
in a pan the size of a dustbin lid.
The pan had a case, like a guitar; and a strap
to strap it to his back like a busker.
But at that moment it was sizzling and roaring.
As was he, a strenuous chef, and too big
if truth be told for our galley-kitchen.

We were too shy to ask if any of those
sausages, bacon, eggs, mushrooms, fried bread and tomatoes
were for us. We are not vegetarian,
and we were hungry, and the larder and fridge
now empty. It is a wise man, he said at last,
settling himself at our breakfast bar
and making free with the brown sauce,
who owns his own frying pan.

To Leigh Hunt

'I see even now
Young Keats, a flowering laurel on your brow'

Millfield Lane, Hampstead. You shook my hand,
that last time, as Coleridge did just here –
the handshake he said of a dying man,
but today I walked the heath, admired the Turner

and understood the distance I had travelled.
The house is a monument. I went instead
to spend an hour with a slip of a girl
in a damp room, no sheets on the bed

but enough claret inside her to be sure.
Indeed she passed out and I was obliged
to finish by myself. Now I am certain
of nothing but the colour of her eyes.

She will wake to a fever on her skin,
despising the money but pocketing it:
almost a remembrance, to say her name again
and leave a note in her currency.

Leigh, you praised me, half-proud of, half-amazed
at my posthumous reputation –
while you, 'The Spirit of the Age',
wrote yourself into oblivion.

One morning she will come to read 'Bright Star'
and, looking to a critic for the answer,
will find your name, vaguely familiar
though she has not read a word of yours;

and then, in Gittings, her brow will crease
at the time you crowned me with laurel,
a night so warm we wrote beneath the stars –
I blushed at those rhymes, but now they make me smile,

pleased to have been your friend. Remembering
will change her too. Because, I remember
how we meant to look back at that evening –
true success, the two of us together

joking, laughing, batting a late moth
from our faces lit with drink, and then
the Reynolds' girl turning up to flirt with.
We would never be that way again.

I read the girl read further, how you lived
to see your best-seller 'Rimini' dismissed,
and coped with it in your not-so-wedded bliss;
while I, Shelley's Adonais,

lay broken in Rome among the English Poets...

*

Well, we have left the night forest,
The landscaped gardens,
The people.

I don't know your second life;
Only that I am obsessed with water.
I have fed a river
I have walked into an ocean
I have taken the coin of language on my tongue

And everything I was once capable of,
Those even to me miraculous words
Wait in my rapid hand,
And in my little books, to be written.
I will not write them.
I have become a reader of water,
A life of sensations.

I have found my place
In the bright book of the dead
Where I sit before a window
Which opens on a lake,
And like the picture of somebody reading
I read daylong, nightlong,

In sunlight that writes itself in water.

Interval

Four myth figure poems for younger readers

Icarus

Daedalus and his son, that parable,
forget it.
It's not about flying too high
but about flying at all.

The son died.
The father lived with his remorse.
Tell me which you think is worse.

Do you really think that ingenious father
imagined for a moment that wax would do?
That man used glue.

Do you really think, as the son got close to the sun
the wax melted
the wings fell apart
and he fell through all those storeys of blue
into the sea?

No. The father knew,
as Icarus would too
before he grew much older,
that as he soared up higher
the air got colder.

Not warmth took the flying out of that boy.
Not warmth but ice on the wings
brought him down
brought him spiralling down

where he belonged.

Prometheus

There was a man
being eaten by a vulture.

The vulture did not clop its beak
round the man's eyeball
and wrench the eye from its socket
to roll it like a nut
staring out for a moment
before he ate it;

it did not tear off the juicy slug
of the man's lower lip
swallow it down
and come back for the other;

it didn't ice-pick its talons
in his skull and rip
at the fleshy ear;

it didn't slice to bacon rind the man's nose
and slurp it in;

it didn't snip off his fingers and toes,
and have them later, like marshmallows;

it left his pumping sweetmeat heart alone.

All the vulture did
was eat the man's liver.

And the man did not die
because each night the liver grew back.
Then in the morning the vulture
would begin again at the liver.

And so on. And so forth.

The man was in agony.

The Minotaur Hadn't Slept for a Week

He lay on his bed of straw, grainy-eyed,
ravenous.

Six years, eleven months three weeks and six days
he'd fasted.

He was not a bull
to be led by the nose out to pasture.
He was not a man
to stroll into town for his dinner.

Flesh of man's flesh, the Minotaur ate
and his gorge rose, later,
at that appetite.

He lived alone, a rumoured creature
in saltmines under the city.
He lived alone.

Every seven years he had company.
But not for long
and they never came back

except in the dreams when they came to him
except in the long hot vivid hungry dreams.

Sisyphus and his stone

he rolled it uphill
it rolled back down again

he rolled it in panic
he rolled it in dread
in stripey pyjamas
he rolled it in bed

he rolled it a house
he rolled it a job
he swaggered it up
to a punch in the gob

he rolled it a wife
a dog at his slipper
he rolled it to Blackpool
and off the big dipper

it fell in a trolley
that rolled down the rows
of ice-cream and tinned peas
in kwiksave & tescos

he rolled it next door
and down to the pub
it rolled along blotto
and starting to blub

he rolled it sad
he rolled it happy
tucked into a pram
and filling its nappy

where it rolled up roses
and bound to go far
to the top of the tree
in a company car

he rolled it up hill
he rolled it up hill
he rolled it up hill
he rolled it up hill

and when he could roll it no longer

it rolled back down again

2

What the Eye Doesn't See

The stationary train that pulls out of a station.
A harbour and island getting underway
across an estuary and out to open sea.
A church moving, as you walk, on the horizon.

The ceiling turning round a single, drunken
lightbulb; or, from a spin in an office chair,
watching the room like a rubber band unwind
to bring the world back to where you were.

A face smiling as you smile only to be kind.
Copying a yawn, limp, twitch or gesture.
Stage-coach wheels turning backwards out of sight.

The flickerbook's lion eating its tamer.
Wind through young wheat making a river.
And who it was forded that water tonight.

Poem

He sat up late, reading
till he was dreaming the story.
Still warm and the scent of the lawn
he'd cut that afternoon. The square of sky
only now properly dark with two or three stars
that shimmered through flaws in the glass.
Above him, she took off her make-up
in the mirror, ran the tap briefly,
the water precious that summer.
He yawned. A general feeling of well-being.
A year from now, she would be with someone else
and so would he. It was midnight,
then it was one. The cat asked to go out;
asked to come back in.
He read to the end of the chapter
marked his place with a cancelled ticket,
turned everything off, and went up to her.

A Walk

In the valley, a train makes its way
into the distance. We are going for a walk
because if you stay in all day you feel bad.
Nothing had prepared me and everything
that I remembered spooled back into itself.
My friend has rung about his marriage,
a situation anyone could have foreseen.

We go down the shifting track to the canal
that is stopped at the choked-up lock
and though we cast bread toward the reeds
the mallard we know are there won't come for it.
The time of year, we surmise, walking further,
throwing more bread, they have young ones, or eggs,
we'll have to buy a book on it.

[Insert Title]

If you help me
I can see [insert details] from here
through the fuzzy [insert details]
I hold to my eyes. Swing through

forty-five degrees, and there it is:
[insert details]. Remember

those afternoons we'd cycle as far as [details]
for no better reason than [details].
I recall best the pedal
ready to take my weight, the setting off.

That and actually [details].
And us at that midnight picnic
when [details], and the unexpected
churchbells. Not to mention the

[details]:
it comes into focus, [details] and [details]
like music/a river in summer/a constellation,
like [details].

The Waitress with an Unwashed Thumb

in the gravy of steak pie and chips
is thirty today if you believe her badge.
She's worked here twenty years to my knowledge.
Above her head the weird blue halo
of an insectocutor. 'You're welcome.'

Her boss is the fattest man I've ever seen;
huge yet somehow only half-inflated.
On the walls are landscapes that might be
lesser-known Constables and down one side
enormous mirrors that do make the room bigger.
The veg is cabbage instead of peas.
You can almost hear the dj's perm
in *All the hits all day long* and the
ceiling fan is at most a week
from bringing itself down.

The hanging plants, mostly fuchsia,
though plastic are not unattractive,
and in an alcove across an embossed ocean
a galleon off a ha'penny makes headway
beside Roman plates in the original colours.
When the song ends an announcement
from Yorkshire Water puts me in mind

of a warm summer midnight,
when, her guests half an hour nearer home
and their plates doing in the dishwasher,

a still fairly young woman
hums Haydn in a peach towelling robe
while hosing her lawn and parched roses
by the yellow light from the kitchen window.

Hardly Worth Mentioning

except there was blood, quite a lot
staining the table beside the coaster
thoughtfully provided, you might have thought,
to rest a cut hand on, gripping the fingers
to staunch it while you worked out what to do.

It didn't seem much, but when I showed them
they were alarmed, said 'Casualty'; and then
my finger, only the little finger actually
of my left hand, lay beside the coaster –
a joke-shop replica, staining the table more.

It didn't hurt. I thought how sharp
the blade must have been, precision-tooled:
I pictured sparks at a whetstone
(though I suppose it was a factory)
and they could think of nothing to say but
'It's serious.' I said, 'Well then, I shall faint'

and did. Their voices reached me
down a corridor of doors that echoed closed
on a picnic with the girl who lost the child
and there was an end of it; and at once
I was back in the office still in this
ludicrous predicament, but now

aware I'd wet myself. 'I will never play
the piano again,' I said and no one laughed.
They took me to the car, talking about shock,
and with my finger in a Strepsils tin.
'They'll sew it back on,' they said;
'they can do it really easily these days.'

They couldn't though. Look.

The Grant

He could join them at a peppercorn rent
until March or possibly April. Time enough
the letter said to finish his project.
But the work, put off till spring,
would be done too late or never done.
He had had the grant, not inconsiderable
and long since spent. The yellow daybed
looked out on a factory that all summer
men dismantled to its tentpole girdering,
two men in hard hats, shorts and trainers,
high enough, walking that shell
upright, casual, tanned, that should they
and their monkey wrench, their clawhammer
fall, no doubt about it they would die.
Meanwhile, twice a week a bulldozer
kept the yard tidy, and all day
a bonfire of that once workplace burned
in a corner of the potholed carpark.

In such a way art or science is furthered –
the break-throughs made that no one wants,
experiments brought to their inconclusion;
and portraits hung on the wall of a gallery
that only those depicted visit: to praise,
for a time, in place, with reason.

Today We Are Shooting Poets

not bad or good poets
not metrical, not free verse not concrete
or performance poets,
not poets who write about nothing but poetry and poets,

not confessional poets,
English but like pop groups singing in American,

not poets writing as if they were talking as if
anyone ever talked like that,

not poets who write about what it is
never to be able to write, or love poems
or sex poems or poems about the colour of
their oppression or about the gender
of their oppression or about its class,

not poets with words all
over the place and lowercase i's,
not incomprehensible even to themselves poets

not poets who get famous for something
be it poetry or who they are or what they do
besides writing poems

not neglected poets
nor the experts on their own poems
who ready nobody for fear of influence,

not poets up to the ears in scholarship
and not a spark in them

no. We are shooting the other poets.
You know who they are and I do.
Let's go buddy, let's do it.

I Am Travelling

I am travelling,
and you are waiting in a buffet;
you are reading

a better class of pulp
a book that sold a million
a book that changes lives

and you've just worked out
that that shikashikashi
is Mozart in a walkman.

I am travelling
while you cool your heels
in the concourse of an open station.

I am travelling.
And later, when at intervals
they've funnelled in

unstoppable smiles
running for buses
or queuing for taxis

and you've checked the last possible time
and given it ten minutes
and another ten,

till there's only
the midnight thirty to Paignton
and my *plenty of tape*

after the tone;
and you've walked up alone
too late for the pub and late-night offy,

I might phone your place
to apologize, to give you
my apologies.

But no excuses.
There is no reason,
no perfectly simple

explanation.
I am travelling.
I am travelling.

Off-Peak Single to Wakefield Westgate

First the world I know well, the Leeds line
past scrub and willowherb, parallel
to the canal I cycle daily. A jackdaw
scooting into feathery grass disproves
itself. Deighton, and stumps of chimneys
with today a 50ft ladder and a steeplejack,
building. Already the canal and river
at Colne Bridge. Then toward Mirfield:
hills are rich slag opened by mammoth JCB's;
slate warehouse roofs store tumbledown light.
On the left the sky in a clean mirror
darkens before a weir yellow with pollutant.
Also, a mill tower serrated with birds,
pigeons I shouldn't wonder; and a park:
playing fields where runners improve slowly.
High octane tankers corroded through, and,
hardly there at all, an ochre pleasure boat.
Next what was Thornhill Power Station, its
insides ripped out: one-dimension, outfaced
by a church making hosiery. Listen, one silent
emulsion-white dome, then a farmhouse with a
lean-to roof and a kid whooping his arms
through this mizzling afternoon in the holidays.
These things: a second sewerage farm;
lorries of soft margarine; a crane over
a factory; a Capri on its uppers;
crows on telegraph wires; a junction
of tons of track, two stationary engines
and assorted rolling stock. A man and a man
on crutches welding a door with sparks,
followed slowly by a goat; a belfry; blocks
of private garages and a flooded field on which
ducks drag fishing-line v's. A golf course
and a graveyard fronted by washing; Wakefield
Cathedral turning into view, and cooling towers;
the empty structure of a gasworks;
a worsted spinners. Finally the city
where we met those years ago, the left-over rust
of Wakefield Kirkgate and backwards then,
some of the same made different, facing
the wrong way, off the branch line to the
prizewinning hanging-baskets of Wakefield Westgate.

The Liverpool to Leeds Passes
Colne Bridge at 04:04

And beyond the darkness beyond the bedside lamp
a kaleidoscope of sounds comes (in summer) across
a cricket pitch in darkness; a canal
flooded suddenly with moonlight; across
a swollen river – the Colne moments before it
becomes the Calder – ; across marshland
owned by Yorkshire Water, and a steep road where
the streetlighting ends.

                    Up the ginnel the sound comes
very fast indeed, bouncing off the outhouse and the 12ft
gritstone wall that keeps the hill from
toppling into my front room/kitchen. There it is.
And up there too. Then the blue, orchard
moonlight subsides behind cloud; and our dark hemisphere
is, when I put down
the dog-eared Penguin Andrew Marvell
and switch off the light and close my eyes,

the inside of a canoe hoisted upturned
on the head of a salmon fisher who drags mile
after mile himself and his shadow like an exhausted friend
across this difficult terrain to the river
and I can tell in the way one always can
that they are right to fear they're hopelessly lost.

In Not More Than Words,
How Is The World Like An Apple?

Here is an apple like a tennis ball.
A red tennis ball.
New apples, please.

My husband has fallen from the apple tree.
My husband/wife has fallen/falls/will fall from the apple/pear tree.

Hello, she said at last, my name is Eve.
Hello, not to be outdone, I'm Isaac.
Here is the apple with its friends the apples.
This is called windfall.
This is called fruitbowl.
I am a cox's, what are you please?
I am pippin, many thanks.

The world is like an apple because you can peel it.
The world is like an apple because you can juggle it with the two
        other worlds.
The world is like an apple because of cider.

Sketch for an English Nature Poem

My resolve is not what it was, a sunset posted in one climate, arriving smudged by another. I closed it as a bookmark in a story I was living for a friend: in those days I'd read the books and he'd do the garden, decorate, and mend whatever broke down. Give and take, like a marriage. He never complained, either, though often enough I got the stories wrong, that happy-ending, that Now A Major Film. But today, looking from the upstairs of a manor house over acres of woodsmoke, russet and privilege, I saw again it was a Hardy novel, not *Look Back In Anger*. I wasn't appalled. I was warmed by it, like seeing the glow through trees of a window where a woman sits reading. And here I am, looking out on all this, as if it were ours. As if someday it might be. I note that the sun on the far hills is to morning like old age is to childhood. I notice the woods with their late birdsong. The woman turns a page, wondering about a pot of tea. Then I open the book and there she is, her place marked exactly, her life stopped mid-sentence by this card and the cello sonata a teenager is murdering downstairs.

Of the Masses

They lived here. It was an estate
like many another. In winter
the thin houses, paths were death-traps.
Some weeks in summer people turned brown
and laughed in the face of the government.

They worked on an industrial estate,
remembering the Clyde and Mersey.
In autumn the upturned soil of roadworks
and a window in the weather
seeded poppy. In June fields of wheat

turned red between estates; in October
that gorgeous weed was harvested.

*

Catherine Cookson/the Doomsday Book,
the cross/the cross my palm for luck
the nothing succeeds like success
the wildflower meadows with no access,
the young who had it handed on a plate,
the scroungers living off the state,
the satelite dish/the beer and fags
the videos/the next home match
the fortnight in caravans
the fortnight in caravans
the ironing/the shopping list,
the velvet glove/the iron fist
the pushchairs and the high-chairs
the rolling pins/the mothers-in-law
the milkmen and the her-next-doors
the prefab clubs/the real pub grub/
the false call and the eyes down/
the line call and the eyes down
for a full house
of fiction and the real estate.

Poem

An ordinary day, three mile tail back
out of Mossley. A woman with a headscarf;
a woman in a leopardskin coat and heels;
a woman with a pushchair; a woman dragging
a squatting dog past a chemists; a woman
with a shopping bag. And also a priest,
crossing in and out of the stopped river
of traffic. The long coat with the hood up
gets him called Monk, but he's a priest,
or was. I heard him a few times years ago:
an uncle's wedding, somebody's christening,
and our Gwen put away with the wrong name.
There he is, large as life, talking as usual,
the way they do. Now we are moving again.
I get into second before he can bless me
and am off then at least as far as the lights.

The Sunset like a Huge Bonfire

is actually a huge bonfire.
The village are burning doors.
Front doors, mainly.
You can see them now, two or
three to an awkward or heavy door,
a man with a door
balanced on his head,
doors on prams, two brothers
with their father's door between them
up to the already burning doors.
Garden gates went last year,
and leaving their doors ajar
was an insufficient gesture:
a small step, then,
to this twilight ritual.
The more enthusiastic
are carting living room and kitchen doors.
A woman there has a serving hatch under her arm.
Others are at cupboards and cabinets
or unscrewing the fitted wardrobe.
It's true that not all the doors
are going to the flames,
but then the fire is not the point.
Some just can't do it, like the man
in his yard knocking up a lean-to.
There are doors just lying around
or propped against walls.
There are doors neatly stacked
waiting for a purpose.
But now there are doorways
where there were doors.
With no thought for theft or winter
these neighbours pass
under their open lintels, they cross
their thresholds unhindered.
The blue front door
lying on next door's lawn
is a puzzle no longer.
It opens to the aluminium rungs
of a short descent
into solid darkness, from which,
the woman in the papershop says,

we will all one day return.
I see myself coming up there,
blinking, shading my eyes.
For now, I take a lumphammer
to the windowframes,
as careful as I can be of the glass.

Autobiography

I have read this page before
and go on reading it, the same page.
I know it by heart and yet
the surprise is I always forget:
and turn the page on to the same page
until I cannot read any more.

From my armchair the fields and roads
flash past, too quick to recognize,
too many to count. It is a sort of progress
to have left behind the fields and roads,
and to look out from my chair by the fire
across a landscape flat as water,
which cormorant, gannet, gull and heron
trawl over, dawn to dusk to dawn,
or land on without ripple or reflection.

Bliss

Only laziness held him back. He could do
anything, when in that instant it seemed
there was no time. In the tin-hut Sunday School
he'd learned three score and ten, like all of us,
but he was shortchanged by tachycardia.
Beneath him the green rich-watered lawn,
the tattered banana tree, the frangipani's
dropped, still-dropping, single sweet flower
by his as yet undiscovered death;
all of it brighter than real, and seen by him
from above, like a film he thought
but no, more like a scene in the novel
the film is based on. Thirty feet up,
weightless, he stopped, not floating,
just being there. Though he always laughed
at the idea of an hereafter, the phrase
'Waiting for admittance' occurred to him:
a line in a song he knew the sense of
and the music, but not the words.

He looked round, it might be the last time
and, though his bifocals lay on the lawn
beside his book and body, he saw easily
the new estate: house upon house at which
Jimbo with that dog of his delivered
the late papers; and there was Mrs Deidre
hacking at her columbine; and there was Peter;
but mostly he saw their own verandah
where his friends and his wife were not panicked
or thinking differently about him, and no one
had rung for an ambulance. From this angle
how clearly he could read their shapes,
a language he had never known before,
the chiming just-touched wine-glasses,
the loose neckline of his wife's blouse
and how it was he'd come to marry her.
It struck him he could be here a long time,
his head filling with music, the soundtrack
to what he could see of everyone,

except it was not played music, but heard
the way some people can read a score
and hear it in their heads, and who therefore
never hear quite that music at all.

An Angel

A disappointment to be
like I was on earth, except
for the uniform – charcoal grey,
white shirt, royal blue tie –
and being insubstantial.
Everyone here is insubstantial
except when we touch.

This was enough for a while,
a phrase which has no meaning here.
It is historical or present time:
I have narrowed the days down
to an infinite number.
Then we are told it is London.

I suppose it is
though I did not know London well.
If you are tired of London
the manager quite seriously said.
It could be anywhere;
there is no door, and the windows
are high in the walls, like first school.

We see daylight. Clouds.
We see rain. English rain I suppose
which not so far away falls
on the Thames. I listen
for traffic or music or voices
but it is a silent London
beyond the window, the stone walls.
There is no-one here and there is everyone.

I sit with my knees drawn up
to my chin as yesterday
and the day before.
But today they have brought us work.
For idle hands, as he says, always,
and because it will set us free.
I took this literally
though this place is not a prison.
I wouldn't want you to think it is a prison.

At the End of Here

you might imagine them as they cluster
shivering on the near bank, waiting for the ferry.
Already they are not people but exhibits.
They are saying their lost causes, their successes,
and it is a museum, this sloping shingle beach
out of season, without visitors, except themselves,
and unaware of each other; which is as well
for they are pitifully naked
beside the deserted funfair, the boarded-up arcade,
the crescent of hotels still with winter lettings,
air-conditioning and a sea-view
to every room, like the one we look out from.
It is not night as you expected.
And now, as a liner appears on the horizon,
it is warmer, and filling slowly with colour.
You can see them quite clearly, though distant,
despite the sea-fret. You can see their faces.
Are there any there you recognize?
Take a good long look. It is difficult, I know,
not least because
though they got up from their graves to be here,
though they unburned and remade themselves to wait
for a short journey by water, across some river
whose name if asked is on the tip of their tongue,
you notice that they are none of them as they were,
you notice they are all of an age,
in their prime, in their twenties,
even the senile, even the cot-death,
and as it were with all their lives before them.

Whitby

1

I woke in the middle of my days
still wearing those off-white cords
and with a three-day beard and a tune
in my head from a party I left early.
Look at my hands. Look what I have done
to them, all those things I had them carry.
It will be different now, I said, finding
a kettle and a toaster, and opening a tin
for the cat that seems to live here.
The salt in the air even before the view
told me it was the coast.

Which is how I come to sit in this high room,
though I could go higher, and look out
on three sides round at town, sea and harbour,
and the southern face of a redbrick townhouse
whose Georgian windows send back pantile roofs
and I know that nothing is finally accounted for,
just as when a lamp is lighted this evening
the outside in those windows will give place
to a living-room like a gallery. I know it
and I know it, as they say, on the pulse.
For a moment I might be in that room,
my fingers drag through dust on a bureau,
or I lay wood and coal in a stone fireplace,
or gaze out at these two rented storeys,
delighting in change; though I know too
with change what must follow. Follow I mean
for example in the way in the harbour
that sea bird depends on its skimming shadow
or the way the wake of a herring-boat breaks
and is spent still in mid-channel.

2

Down there, the harbour is oil, in which
spilt lights are broken and healed over,
broken; houselights and two-hundred steps up
the floodlit church laid out in a yellow splodge,
somewhere between primrose and umber.
Walk further, through the stale smell of fresh fish
where tied-up herring-boats are slack
in the water: coils of rope, diesel, grease;
and the green stern light one brilliant splash.

3

Stillest at night and, except the air
is thick with salt, it could be a simple river.
It is, even though the moon above it
fails to light the landscape it feeds
black as far as the eye can see, and beyond,
where everything that moves delights in change,
slow lights move right to left, south to north,
trawler, ferry, or another boat coming home,

which at length, dawdling, is let run
with the tide, then brought round at the quay
by a bubbling throttle. Dead-calm, sloppy,
this water is to the sea beyond the bar
like dusk-heightened streetlights are
to the same lights at midnight, each route
and dwelling in the town replaced by distance
which the night has made a collar of jewels.

291									
301	302	303	304	305	306	307	308	309	300
311	312	313	314	315	316	317	318	319	310
321	322	323	324	325	326	327	328	329	320
331	332	333	334	335	336	337	338	339	330
341	342	343	344	345	346	347	348	349	340
351	352	353	354	355	356	357	358	359	350
361	362	363	364	365	366	367	368	369	360
371	372	373	374	375	376	377	378	379	370
381	382	383	384	385	386	387	388	389	380
391	392	393	394	395	396	397	398	399	390
									400